This book belongs to:

Evan Gensch

It was given to me by:

SUMC Preschool

On this date:

June 10, 2022

D1316416

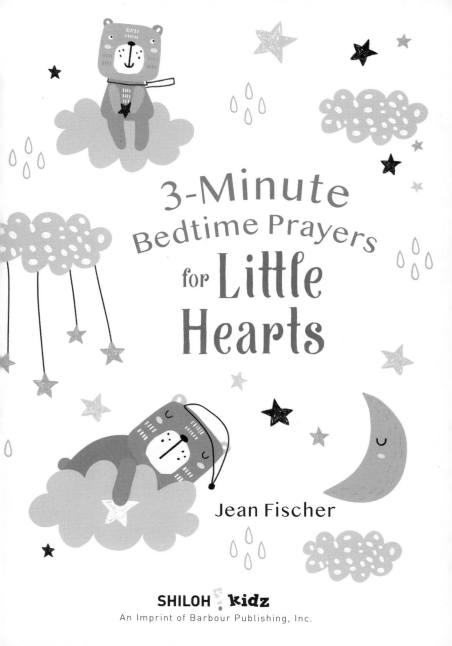

3-Minute
Bedtime Prayers
for Little
Hearts

Jean Fischer

SHILOH kidz
An Imprint of Barbour Publishing, Inc.

ISBN 978-1-64352-281-4

Published by Shiloh Kidz, an imprint of Barbour Publishing, Inc., 1810 Barbour Drive, Uhrichsville, Ohio 44683, www.shilohkidz.com

Our mission is to inspire the world with the life-changing message of the Bible.

Member of the
Evangelical Christian
Publishers Association

Printed in China.
06716   1219   DS

To my mother,
who taught me to pray.

*Through [God's] shining-greatness
and perfect life, He has given us promises.
These promises are of great worth and
no amount of money can buy them.*

2 PETER 1:4

Contents

INTRODUCTION

Everything in the Bible Is True

*Open my eyes so that I may
see great things from Your Law.*
PSALM 119:18

Dear God, thank You for the Bible. It is filled with stories about how You help the people who love You. The Bible's words remind me that You love me and will help me every day, wherever I am. Best of all, the Bible is filled with promises that are for me—right now. So teach me about Your promises, God. I want to learn about them and live my life trusting in each one. Amen.

―――――― **Think about it!** ――――――

Why is it important to read the Bible?

GOD MADE ME

God Created Me

"Before I started to put you together in your mother, I knew you. Before you were born, I set you apart as holy. I chose you to speak to the nations for Me."
JEREMIAH 1:5

Dear God, help me to remember that You made me. Before I was born, even before You put my body together, You knew all about me. You planned what I would look like, where I would live, and all the people I would ever meet. You knew my favorite colors and what I would be really good at. Best of all, God, You made me to be Yours, always and forever. Thank You! Amen.

—— **Think about it!** ——

What do you like best about the way God created you?

I Am a Gift from God

See, children are a gift from the Lord.
The children born to us are our special reward.
PSALM 127:3

Dear God, I've never thought of myself as a gift, but You say that's what I am. A gift is something special because it is given with love. When You created me, You made me special. You formed my body exactly the way You wanted it to be. Then You put all Your love into me and gave me to my parents. I am their best gift ever! I love You, God. Amen.

—————— **Think about it!** ——————

What makes you special?

God Chose Me

"The Lord your God has chosen you out of all the nations on the earth, to be His own."
Deuteronomy 7:6

Dear God, I feel special when someone chooses me as a friend, and I feel extra special knowing that You chose me to be Yours. You made me so You could love me now and forever. You created me as one of a kind. In the whole world, there is no one just like me. Tonight when I close my eyes to sleep, I will remember that You chose me to be Your own. Good night, God. Amen.

--- **Think about it!** ---

In what ways are you different (and special!) from everyone else?

God Made Me Beautiful

"You are all beautiful, my love. You are perfect."
SONG OF SOLOMON 4:7

Dear God, everything You make is perfect, and that is how You made me. I am Your perfect creation. You made me the way You wanted me to be. And when You finished making me, You looked at me and decided that I was the most beautiful child You had ever seen. You feel that way about me all the time. So help me to remember every day that I am Your beautiful child. Amen.

———————— **Think about it!** ————————

What is your favorite thing about God's creation?

God Gave Me a Beautiful Heart

Your beauty should come from the inside.
It should come from the heart. This is the kind that
lasts. Your beauty should be a gentle and quiet spirit.
In God's sight this is of great worth and no
amount of money can buy it.

1 PETER 3:4

Dear God, when You created me, You gave special attention to my heart. You made it a beautiful place that You can fill with Your love. You have poured so much love in there that I have plenty left over to share with others. Thank You, dear God, for my beautiful heart! I love You so much. Amen.

———————— **Think about it!** ————————

What makes someone's heart beautiful?

God's Spirit Lives inside Me

Do you not know that your body is a house of God where the Holy Spirit lives? God gave you His Holy Spirit. Now you belong to God. You do not belong to yourselves. God bought you with a great price. So honor God with your body. You belong to Him.
1 CORINTHIANS 6:19–20

Dear God, I know that You love me and that You are with me all the time. The Bible says that Your Spirit lives inside me. I have trouble imagining that sometimes. But I know that You are God, and that means You can go anywhere and do anything. Remind me to keep my body healthy and clean so it is a nice place for You to live in. Amen.

—————————— **Think about it!** ——————————

How does it feel to know you belong to God?

I Am Important to God

"Are not two small birds sold for a very small piece of money? And yet not one of the birds falls to the earth without your Father knowing it. God knows how many hairs you have on your head. So do not be afraid. You are more important than many small birds."
MATTHEW 10:29–31

Dear God, I am amazed that You can see everything, everywhere, all the time. How do You do that? You see everything that happens. I must be really important for You to always be watching me. You want to know everything about me and everything I do. The Bible says that You even know how many hairs are on my head! Thank You for taking such good care of me, God. I'll see You in the morning. Amen.

———————— **Think about it!** ————————

In what ways does God take care of you?

God Knows My Name

*"Be happy because your
names are written in heaven."*
LUKE 10:20

Dear God, when You look down at me from heaven, You know exactly who I am. I'm not just a kid in a crowd. I'm Yours! You know my name. Whenever You hear my name, it sounds like music to Your ears. You love saying it. The Bible says You even wrote my name in Your book in heaven. It makes me happy that You know my name. I love You, God! Amen.

——————— **Think about it!** ———————

How does it feel to know that
God delights in you, His child?

I Am Alive Because of God

*"It is in Him that we live and move and
keep on living. Some of your own men have
written, 'We are God's children.' "*
ACTS 17:28

Dear God, I know that everything that lives is alive because of You. All the people and all the animals on earth live because You made them. You give life to the birds in the sky, bugs that crawl, and fish in the sea. Flowers, grass, bushes, trees—everything that grows, grows because of You. You give life to everything! Thank You, God, for the gift of living. Thank You for making us all. Amen.

—————— **Think about it!** ——————

What is the most amazing animal God created and why?

God Has Planned All My Days

Your eyes saw me before I was put together.
And all the days of my life were written in Your
book before any of them came to be.

PSALM 139:16

Dear God, before You made me and gave me my body, You had already planned all my days. I have to wait to see what happens, but You already know. You know everything about me today, tomorrow, and always. Help me to remember that. I'm excited to find out what You have planned for me. I wonder: What will I be when I grow up? What will I look like? I can't wait to find out. Amen.

Think about it!

What do you want to be when you grow up and why?

We Are All God's Children

See what great love the Father has for us that He would call us His children. And that is what we are. For this reason the people of the world do not know who we are because they did not know Him.

1 JOHN 3:1

Dear God, it's wonderful that we are all Your children: every kid, mom, dad, grandma, grandpa, aunt, uncle, and cousin—all the people on earth are Yours. That's why we call You our heavenly Father. I'm thankful that You love us all, watch over us, and help us to be the best we can be. You know what we want, and You always give us what we need. I'm glad that I'm Your kid. Amen.

—————— **Think about it!** ——————

How does God provide for your needs?

GOD GAVE ME JESUS!

God Sent Us Jesus

"For God so loved the world that He gave His only Son. Whoever puts his trust in God's Son will not be lost but will have life that lasts forever."
JOHN 3:16

Dear God, sometimes it is hard for people to do what is right. You knew that, so You sent Your Son, Jesus, to help us. You sent Jesus to teach us to be right and good. You sent Him to be with us all the time, now and forever. Best of all, Jesus will lead us to heaven someday. Thank You, God, for giving us Jesus. He is the best Gift of all. Amen.

Think about it!

Why is Jesus the best Gift?

God Will Help Me to Know Jesus

Learn to know our Lord Jesus Christ better.
He is the One Who saves.
2 PETER 3:18

Dear God, I want to know all about Jesus. Open my heart to let Him in. Teach me about Him through the Bible and wherever I go—at home, school, church, and play. I know that Jesus is real. He is my friend. Jesus is with me all the time, and I can depend on Him. I want to trust Jesus and become more like Him every day. Please help me to know Him better. Amen.

—————————— **Think about it!** ——————————

In what ways do you depend on Jesus?
Is He your very best Friend?

Jesus Wants to Live with Me

*"See! I stand at the door and knock.
If anyone hears My voice and opens
the door, I will come in to him."*
REVELATION 3:20

Dear Jesus, I want You to live in my heart so You can be with me forever. I can imagine my heart is like a house with a door. I can think of You knocking on the door and calling my name. All I have to do is open the door and invite You inside. Will You come into my heart right now, Lord Jesus? I want You to live with me now and forever. Amen.

Think about it!

Is Jesus in your heart?

Jesus Loves Children

He took the children in His arms.
He put His hands on them and prayed
that good would come to them.
MARK 10:16

Dear Jesus, You love kids. I know because the Bible says so. When You lived here on earth, You wanted the children to come to You. You held them in Your arms, and You prayed for them. Today, You live in the hearts of everyone who believes in You. It makes me happy knowing that You live in my heart and that You will help with whatever I do. I love You, Jesus! Amen.

———————————— **Think about it!** ————————————

How does it feel to know that Jesus loves kids?

Jesus Helps Me with Everything

I can do all things because
Christ gives me the strength.
PHILIPPIANS 4:13

Dear Jesus, You are my helper. You help me be strong whenever I feel weak. When I think that I can't do something, You help me to try anyway. If I fail, You help me to try again. When something is difficult and I want to give up, You give me strength to keep on going. I am never alone, Jesus, because You are always with me and helping me. Thank You so much! Amen.

─────────── **Think about it!** ───────────

In what ways has Jesus helped you
get through something hard?

Jesus Strengthens My Faith

*Let us keep looking to Jesus. Our faith
comes from Him and He is the
One Who makes it perfect.*
HEBREWS 12:2

Dear Jesus, faith means always believing in God's promises. And sometimes it means waiting for God to do something. That's not easy. But, Jesus, You are my helper. When I need more faith, I know that I can call on You. I believe that God is always with me and doing what is right. So help me, please, to be patient and trust with my whole heart, soul, and mind. Amen.

—————— **Think about it!** ——————

Do you know God's promises
are true? Why or why not?

Jesus Gives Me Power

But we have power over all these things through Jesus Who loves us so much.
Romans 8:37

Dear Jesus, I believe that You can do anything! So with You as my partner, I have power to face whatever seems hard. I want to remember that we do everything together. Trusting in You gives me courage. If I say, "No, I can't," You say, "Yes, you can!" You are my best friend, Jesus. Thank You for sharing Your power with me, for loving me all the time, and for always believing in me. Amen.

--- **Think about it!** ---

What big things could you
accomplish with help from God?

Jesus Helps Me Rest

"Come to Me, all of you who work and have heavy loads. I will give you rest."
MATTHEW 11:28

Dear Jesus, when it is bedtime, I don't always feel like going to bed. I am wide awake, and I want to stay up and play. But rest is important. Rest keeps my body healthy and strong. So, Jesus, when bedtime comes, I will try to go happily. When I say my prayers, please remind me that You will watch over me all night long. Then help me to close my eyes and sleep. Amen.

--- **Think about it!** ---

Why is rest important?

Jesus Wants Me to Have a Great Life

*"I came so they might have life,
a great full life."*
JOHN 10:10

Dear Jesus, trying to please God helps me to live a great life. When I behave in ways that are good, caring, kind, and loving, that makes God happy. And when I follow the rules, He likes that too. Jesus, You are the best example of how to behave, and You want my life to be awesome. I want to please God all the time, so will You teach me to be more like You? Amen.

—————————— **Think about it!** ——————————

What kind of behavior is pleasing to God?

29

Jesus Is My Way to Heaven

Jesus said, "I am the Way and the Truth and the Life. No one can go to the Father except by Me."
JOHN 14:6

Dear God, You think of everything. You want Your children to live with You in heaven someday when their lives here on earth are done. People can't get to heaven by themselves. So You sent Jesus to show us the way. If we trust and believe in Him now, then someday we will live with You and Jesus in heaven. Thank You, God, for Your perfect plan. Thank You for sending us Jesus. Amen.

―――――――――― **Think about it!** ――――――――――

What do you think heaven is like?

Jesus Has a Place for Me in Heaven

"There are many rooms in My Father's house. If it were not so, I would have told you. I am going away to make a place for you."
JOHN 14:2

Dear God, I think heaven must be huge if there is enough space for all of us to live there someday. Jesus loves us so much that He has already made a place for us when we get there. God, I know that it might be a very long time before I see You in heaven, but I'm grateful that You have a new home waiting for me there. I love You, God. Amen.

———————— **Think about it!** ————————

How big do you think heaven is?

Jesus Rules the World

"In the world you will have much trouble.
But take hope! I have power over the world!"
JOHN 16:33

Dear Jesus, parents rule the house. Teachers rule in school. Presidents and kings rule over countries, and generals rule armies. But You are more powerful than all of them put together because You rule the world. You are the King of kings and everyone else! Best of all, Your decisions are always kind and fair. Whenever I feel powerless, I know that I can count on You. Help me to remember that, please. Amen.

—————————— **Think about it!** ——————————

How powerful is God?

Jesus Is for Everyone

God does not see you as a Jew or as a Greek.
He does not see you as a servant or as a person
free to work. He does not see you as a man or
as a woman. You are all one in Christ.
GALATIANS 3:28

Dear Jesus, I belong to You and God, and that's why You love me so much. It doesn't matter the color of my eyes, hair, or skin. Whether I am short or tall, young or old, or where I live isn't important. You love all of God's children just the same! Jesus, I want to love everyone all the time just the way that You do. Will You help me to do that? Amen.

———— **Think about it!** ————

Who does God love?

Jesus Is Forever

*"After I go and make a place for you,
I will come back and take you with Me.
Then you may be where I am."*
JOHN 14:3

Dear Jesus, I know You will never leave me. You promise to be with me here on earth and someday in heaven. Your Spirit is with me all the time, living inside my heart. Every day that I'm here on earth, You watch over me and help me. I can talk with You when I pray and You hear me. Jesus, You and I are forever! That is the best promise of all. Amen.

——————————— **Think about it!** ———————————

How long is forever?

GOD IS THE GREATEST!

God's Promises Never Fail

"Know in all your hearts and in all your souls that not one of all the good promises the Lord your God made to you has been broken. All have come true for you. Not one of them has been broken."

Joshua 23:14

Dear God, I love learning about Your promises. I am finding out that the Bible is filled with them, and all of them are good. Every one of Your promises is true and perfect. One of the best things about You is that You are always trustworthy. I know that when You make a promise, You will keep it. God, help me to be more like You. I want to keep my promises too. Amen.

Think about it!

How many promises does God keep—
just a few. . .or ALL of them?

God Is the Great, Forever King

We give honor and thanks to the King Who lives forever. He is the One Who never dies and Who is never seen. He is the One Who knows all things. He is the only God. Let it be so.
1 TIMOTHY 1:17

Dear God, the Bible says that You are the King of everything. I can't see You, but You are all around me ruling the world. It says that You will live forever and that You know everything. No human king is like You or could ever do what You do. That's because You are God—the one and only God. Thank You for watching over me, knowing all about me, and loving me so much. Amen.

--------- **Think about it!** ---------

If God knows "everything," what kinds of things does He know?

No One Can Completely Understand God

God's riches are so great! The things He knows and His wisdom are so deep! No one can understand His thoughts. No one can understand His ways.
ROMANS 11:33

Dear God, I have so many questions about You. Why can't I see You? What do You look like? How can You know everything about everybody all the time? Some things about You are just too great for humans to understand. I believe that You love me and that You will always take care of me. Help me to trust You even when there is so much that I don't understand. Good night, God. I love You. Amen.

—— **Think about it!** ——

What kinds of questions would you ask God if you could talk to Him face-to-face?

God Is Everywhere

*He is the One Who makes the mountains
and the wind. He makes His thoughts known
to man. He turns the morning into darkness,
and walks on the high places of the earth.
The Lord God of All is His name.*

AMOS 4:13

Dear God, the earth is so big. Still, You are everywhere right now. You are with me and also with every other child in the world—You are with everyone. You are in the fields, forests, deserts, jungles, and even in places that are frozen and cold. You are up in the sky among the stars and the clouds and in the deepest oceans. How do You do that, God? I think You are amazing. Amen.

—————————— **Think about it!** ——————————

Where is God?

God Knows Everything

*"For My thoughts are not your thoughts, and
My ways are not your ways," says the Lord.
"For as the heavens are higher than the earth,
so are My ways higher than your ways, and
My thoughts than your thoughts."*
ISAIAH 55:8–9

Dear God, I want to remember that You always do what is best for me. You know everything that goes on with me and what I am thinking. You might not always agree with what I want. That is because Your plans for me are better than my own plans. You know exactly what I need. So, if something doesn't go my way and I feel disappointed, please remind me that You know best. Amen.

——————— **Think about it!** ———————

Why are God's plans always best?

God Sees Everything All the Time

*"For He looks to the ends of the earth,
and sees everything under the heavens."*
JOB 28:24

Dear God, You see everything. That makes me feel good because I know that You watch over me. Wherever I go, You see me. If I am at home or at a friend's house, You are there. You see me all the time. Even if I wanted to, I couldn't hide from You. Sometimes, God, I forget that You are watching. Help me to do what is right. I want to please You. Amen.

Think about it!

What can God see?

God Made Everything

He made all things. Nothing was made without Him making it.
JOHN 1:3

Dear God, tonight I want to think about all the wonderful things You have made. You created my family and friends, animals, bugs, birds, the sunshine, and stars. You made the mountains, oceans, and everything that grows. You made me! You gave me my brain that thinks and my hands and feet that allow me to do things. Help me to be thankful for everything You have made and all that You do. Thank You, God. Amen.

Think about it!

Who should receive praise for all the wonderful things in the world?

God Does Great Work

"Stop and think about the great works of God."
JOB 37:14

Dear God, You do such a good job taking care of me. When I stop and think about You, I remember how much You love me. You must be so busy, and still You always have time for me. I feel happy when people tell me that I am doing a good job. So, God, I want to tell You that You are doing a *great* job! I hope that makes You happy. Amen.

—————————— **Think about it!** ——————————

What makes God happy?

God Understands Everything

*His understanding is too great
for us to begin to know.*
ISAIAH 40:28

Dear God, one of the things I love most about You is that You always understand me. Even when my family, friends, or teachers don't understand how I feel, You do. Whether I am happy, sad, grumpy, or giggly, You know exactly what is going on with me. Sometimes I wish that everyone understood me as well as You do. Maybe when they don't seem to understand, You could help them a little bit? Thank You, God. Amen.

Think about it!

Who understands you the best?

God Can Do Anything!

*Jesus looked at them and said,
"This cannot be done by men.
But with God all things can be done."*
MATTHEW 19:26

Dear God, I believe that You are greater and more powerful than anything. You see and hear everything, and You can be everywhere all at the same time. You know things that people can't know, and You have a plan for everything. When I pray, I trust that You hear me and that You will give me what I need. I am grateful that You are *my* God and the one and only God. Amen.

Think about it!

Is there anything God *can't* do?

God Has Power over the Weather

Ask the Lord for rain in the spring time. It is the Lord Who makes the storm clouds. He gives rain to men, and gives vegetables in the field to every one.
ZECHARIAH 10:1

Dear God, there is a story in the Bible about Jesus stopping a big windstorm (Matthew 8:23–27). He stood up and told the wind to stop, and it did! I forget sometimes that You are more powerful than any kind of weather. I promise to thank You for nice, sunny days. And if it rains, I will thank You for giving the earth a drink. When storms come, I know that You will watch over me. Good night, God. Amen.

─────── **Think about it!** ───────

Are you afraid of storms? Why or why not?

God Has Power over Everything

God has power over all things forever.
1 PETER 5:11

Dear God, You are the King of everything. You rule over everyone, and You are a good King! You love us all and want what is best for us. Your rules are perfect and fair. No leader on earth has the power to rule the way that You do. You are great and perfectly powerful all the time, and You are everywhere all the time. God, I feel safe knowing that You are in charge. Amen.

————————— **Think about it!** —————————

What makes God's rules perfect and fair?

God Does What Is Right and Fair

So the Lord wants to show you kindness. He waits on high to have loving-pity on you. For the Lord is a God of what is right and fair. And good will come to all those who hope in Him.
ISAIAH 30:18

Dear God, sometimes You don't answer my prayers the way that I want You to. But I know that I can count on Your kindness. You have a good plan for me. You promise to do what is right and fair. And because You are so wise, You understand what is best for me. Help me to remember that and to continue to trust You, even when You don't give me what I want. Amen.

—————— **Think about it!** ——————

Do you trust God's plan for you? Why or why not?

God Loves What Is Fair and Right

For the Lord loves what is fair and right.
PSALM 37:28

Dear Jesus, You are the best example of what is fair and right. As I learn about You, I see how good You are. You do everything perfectly right. You love everyone all the time, and You love seeing them behaving well and treating others with respect. Jesus, I want to be more like You. Teach me to do what is right. I want to treat people with fairness—the way that You do. Amen.

--------------------- **Think about it!** ---------------------

What makes Jesus a perfect example to follow?

God Makes Everything Good

We know that God makes all things work together for the good of those who love Him and are chosen to be a part of His plan.
ROMANS 8:28

Dear God, You promise to work things out. You know how to solve every problem, especially those that seem so tangled there is no way to fix them. Help me to trust in You. When I have a problem, remind me that You might take awhile to work it out—but You always will. I believe that You have a good plan for me, and I know that You will make things right. Amen.

—————— **Think about it!** ——————

Who should you talk to when you have a problem?

God Is Always Faithful

O Lord, Your loving-kindness goes to the heavens. You are as faithful as the sky is high.
PSALM 36:5

Dear God, how much do You love me? The Bible says that Your loving-kindness goes to the heavens. That is higher than the moon and back! You are as faithful as the sky is high. No one knows how high the sky is—no one except You. Your love for me goes all the way up to heaven where You are. Oh, thank You, God, for being so loving, kind, and faithful to me. Amen.

—————————— **Think about it!** ——————————

How much does God love you?

God Is Trustworthy

Every word of God has been proven true.
He is a safe-covering to those who trust in Him.
PROVERBS 30:5

Dear God, Your promises are true—every single one. I know that I can trust You. I can count on You to always be here for me, and I know that You will do what is best for me. I believe that You love me. You are my heavenly Father, the One who never breaks a promise and the One who never lets me down. I trust You, and I love You so much. Amen.

———————— **Think about it!** ————————

How do you know that you can trust God?

God Will Never Lie

"God is not a man, that He should lie."
NUMBERS 23:19

Dear God, when You make a promise, I know I can trust it because You never lie. You tell the truth always. I'm sure that You want me to tell the truth too. You want me to be like Jesus, honest and trustworthy all the time. God, help me to do my best to be truthful. I want my family, teachers, friends—everyone—to trust me. I want You to trust me too. Amen.

——————— **Think about it!** ———————

What makes a person trustworthy?

God Is Good

"O give thanks to the Lord, for He is good.
His loving-kindness lasts forever."
1 CHRONICLES 16:34

Dear God, people aren't perfect. We all make mistakes. That's why You sent Jesus, to forgive our mistakes. If I believe in Him, follow His example, and do my best, then I will please You. Father, I want to do what is right. Remind me of Your goodness. You love me all the time. If I mess up, I know that You will forgive me and help me to do better next time. Thank You, God. Amen.

——————— **Think about it!** ———————

What kinds of mistakes does God
forgive—just some. . .or ALL?

God Is Patient

*But You, O Lord, are a God full of love
and pity. You are slow to anger and
rich in loving-kindness and truth.*
PSALM 86:15

Dear God, how can You be so patient? People must get on Your nerves sometimes. Still, You promise to be slow getting angry. You treat us with love and kindness, even when we don't deserve it. God, I don't always behave my best. But You keep right on being patient with me. I love that about You. Will You help me to be more patient too? Amen.

——————— **Think about it!** ———————

What does it mean to be patient?
And why is it important?

God Is Kind

*The loving-kindness of God
lasts all day long.*
PSALM 52:1

Dear God, I feel loved when someone is kind to me, but I forget sometimes to be kind back. I can show kindness by saying gentle words, being helpful, and also by trying to understand how others feel. How else can I practice kindness, God? Teach me, please. Every day, wherever I go, open my eyes to people who need a little kindness. Then show me how I can help. Good night, God. I love You. Amen.

Think about it!

What does it mean to be kind?
And why is it important?

God's Kindness Is Forever

"The mountains may be taken away and the hills may shake, but My loving-kindness will not be taken from you."
Isaiah 54:10

Dear heavenly Father, You are so perfectly kind, and You have promised never to take Your kindness away from me. You said that no one, nothing at all, can take Your loving-kindness away. Believing that truth helps me to feel happy and safe. Your love and kindness are forever. I can count on them all the days of my life. I think Your promises are wonderful, God. Thank You for them. Amen.

Think about it!

What can you learn from God's kindness?

God Does Not Stay Angry

For His anger lasts only a short time.
But His favor is for life. Crying may last for
a night, but joy comes with the new day.
PSALM 30:5

Dear God, I feel angry sometimes. I get upset and I cry. You see everything, so You already know that about me. You get angry sometimes too. But You promise to stay angry just a little while. I want to be more like You. I don't want to hold on to my angry feelings. So when they stir up inside me, will You help me to let go of them quickly? I'd rather feel happy. Amen.

——————— **Think about it!** ———————

Is it okay to be angry sometimes?

God Never Gets Tired

He will not become weak or tired.
Isaiah 40:28

Dear God, I am ready to go to sleep. I've had a very busy day, and I'm tired. The Bible says that You never sleep. How do You do that? You are busier than anyone I know! I'm glad that You don't get tired, God, because when I lie down to sleep and snuggle under the covers, I feel safe knowing that You are up all night. Thank You for watching over me. I love You. Amen.

───────────── **Think about it!** ─────────────

Does God ever sleep?

God Does Not Change

"For I, the Lord, do not change."
MALACHI 3:6

Dear God, people grow and change, but You don't. You are the same wonderful God all the time. You have promised to stay the same forever. Everything You say, think, and do is perfect, and it will be like that always. I love knowing that You won't change because that means I can count on You and Your promises. When You promise something, I can be sure it is true forever. Thank You, God! Amen.

——————— **Think about it!** ———————

Why is it important that God doesn't ever change?

God Is the God of Everyone!

There is no difference between the Jews and the people who are not Jews. They are all the same to the Lord. And He is Lord over all of them. He gives of His greatness to all who call on Him for help.
ROMANS 10:12

Dear God, when You made people, You made their bodies one of a kind. You chose the color of their skin, eyes, and hair. Some You made girls and others boys. You decided where they would be born. Best of all, You loved them all the same. You don't have favorites, God. You love us all with Your great big forever love. I want to love everyone too. Will You help me, please? Amen.

Think about it!

Why doesn't God have favorites?

No One Is Greater than God

*O Lord my God, many are the great works
You have done, and Your thoughts toward us.
No one can compare with You!*
PSALM 40:5

Dear God, You are so great that no one—not even the smartest people—can know everything about You. Nobody can do what You do. You made mountains and oceans, the sky and stars. The Bible says that You know exactly how many stars there are, and You have names for them all. No one else can count the stars. You are the perfect, one and only God, and I'm grateful that I know You. Amen.

Think about it!

What do you think is the most
amazing, coolest thing about God?

God Is Forever

The Lord God says, "I am the First and the Last, the beginning and the end of all things. I am the All-powerful One Who was and Who is and Who is to come."
REVELATION 1:8

Dear God, please help me to understand that You are forever. You were not born. No one chose You to be God. You have always been God! You are here now, and You will be here forever. You will never end. You made everything. You control everything. You loved me even before I was born, and You promise to love me forever. I like that promise. Dear God, I want to love You forever too. Amen.

—————————— **Think about it!** ——————————

Will God's love for you really
go on forever and ever?

I CAN TALK WITH GOD

God Wants Me to Talk with Him

Never stop praying.
1 Thessalonians 5:17

Dear God, before I go to sleep, I want to thank You for prayers. Praying is how I can talk with You. Since You are with me all the time, I know that I can talk with You wherever I am. I can ask You about anything and tell You about my thoughts and feelings. Whatever I need, I can ask You for it. Thank You for prayers, God, and for listening to me tonight. Amen.

—— **Think about it!** ——

Does God really hear every prayer?

God Teaches Me How to Pray

*"When you pray, go into a room by yourself.
After you have shut the door, pray to your
Father Who is in secret. Then your Father
Who sees in secret will reward you."*
MATTHEW 6:6

Dear God, please help me to set aside some quiet time each day to talk with You. Teach me to pray about everything and ask for whatever I need. Show me that I don't have to use special words when I pray. I can talk with You all the time as if I am talking with my closest friend—because that is who You are, my very best friend. I love You, God. Amen.

——————— **Think about it!** ———————

Where is your favorite place to talk to God?

God Knows What I Need When I Pray

Do not worry. Learn to pray about everything. Give thanks to God as you ask Him for what you need.

PHILIPPIANS 4:6

Dear God, when I pray, I know that I can ask You for whatever I need. I can ask for big things, like help with my problems, and I can ask You for little things too. I understand that sometimes You won't give me exactly what I have asked for. That is because You know better what I need and when I need it. Thank You for always giving me Your best. Good night, God. Amen.

———————— **Think about it!** ————————

Is anything ever too big for God to handle?

God Hears My Prayers

*"Then you will call upon Me and come
and pray to Me, and I will listen to you."*
JEREMIAH 29:12

Dear God, You made a promise to hear my prayers. I like that promise! You hear every word I say. You are never too busy to hear me. Whether I say something simple like, "Good morning, God," or "Good night," You hear my words. You hear me when I tell You my feelings, when I ask for Your help, or when I just want to talk with You. Thank You for hearing me, God. Amen.

—————————— **Think about it!** ——————————

Is God ever too busy to listen to you?

God Listens to Me

My God will hear me.
MICAH 7:7

Dear God, You don't just hear my prayers; You know my voice, and You care what I say. You think about my words. You listen to all my prayers with love. That makes me feel good. You are the very best listener because You always take time to hear me. Please help me to remember that I can pray anytime, anywhere, and You will listen and care about what I say. Thank You for listening tonight. Amen.

———————— **Think about it!** ————————

How many good listeners do you know?

God Will Answer Me

"Call to Me, and I will answer you. And I will show you great and wonderful things which you do not know."

JEREMIAH 33:3

Dear God, You promised to answer my prayers, and I believe in Your promise. Every night, I feel Your love when I'm tucked into bed falling asleep. I know that You heard me praying. You promised to show me great and wonderful things, and I believe that You will. God, help me to listen for Your voice inside my heart. Please help me to notice all the amazing things that You do. Amen.

―――――――――― **Think about it!** ――――――――――

In what ways has God answered your prayers?

God Knows My Prayers Even Before I Say Them

"And it will be before they call, I will answer. While they are still speaking, I will hear."
ISAIAH 65:24

Dear God, how can You know everything before it happens? It is something that only You can do. You like hearing me pray. But before one word leaves my lips, You already know what I will say and how You will answer me. You know me so well. I love it that You know everything that is going on with me, and You have it all under control. I think You are amazing, God! Amen.

———————— **Think about it!** ————————

Who knows you best?

God Helps Us to Pray for Each Other

Christian brothers, pray for us.
1 THESSALONIANS 5:25

Dear God, tonight I ask You to watch over my family and friends. Be with all sick people and those who are worried or unhappy. I want all children in the world to know You like I do, so I pray for them too. Please be a friend to everyone and come into their hearts. And, God, if someone I know needs prayers, tell me about it, so I can pray for them too. Amen.

—————————— **Think about it!** ——————————

Who needs your prayers tonight?

God Teaches Me to Pray for My Enemies

"Respect and give thanks for those who try to bring bad to you. Pray for those who make it very hard for you."
LUKE 6:28

Dear God, some people are hard to pray for. Still, that is what You want me to do. Those people need prayers the most. Help the ones who have hurt my feelings. Teach them to be gentle and kind. If someone is thinking of doing something wrong, lead them to change their minds. Please forgive those who have already done something wrong, and help me to be forgiving too. Remind me, God: You love everybody. Amen.

—————————— **Think about it!** ——————————

Why do hard-to-pray-for people
need your prayers the most?

Praying Will Help Me to Do What Is Right

When He got there, He said to them,
"Pray that you will not be tempted."
Luke 22:40

Dear God, sometimes I do things that I know are wrong. Everyone does. But I know that You are unhappy when I misbehave. I'm sorry. I want to please You. When I feel like doing the wrong thing, if I pray will You help me? I know that I can count on You to make me strong so I will choose the right thing to do. I promise to try my best. Amen.

Think about it!

How does it feel when you
choose to do the right thing?

THE BIBLE IS GOD'S WORD

God Speaks to Me through the Bible

All the Holy Writings are God-given and are made alive by Him. Man is helped when he is taught God's Word. It shows what is wrong. It changes the way of a man's life. It shows him how to be right with God.
2 TIMOTHY 3:16

Dear God, the Bible is a way that You speak to my heart. Your words in the Bible are for everyone. They help us and teach us right from wrong. The Bible will show me how to please You by living the right way. I'm glad that You gave us the Bible! Please lead me to people who will help me to learn and understand its words. Amen.

--- **Think about it!** ---

What is your favorite Bible verse and why?

The Bible Is for Today

God's Word is living and powerful.
HEBREWS 4:12

Dear God, You promised that the words in the Bible are forever. You planned Your words for everyone who would read them. The Bible is for me today, and it is important to know what is in it. I know that I can learn from the Bible about my own life. Your words in the Bible will guide me every day, if I learn and follow them. Help me to do that, God. Amen.

—————————— **Think about it!** ——————————

How can the Bible help you in everyday life?

God Will Help Me Understand the Bible

*Then He opened their minds
to understand the Holy Writings.*
LUKE 24:45

Dear God, some things about You are difficult to understand. You know that, so You gave us the Bible. You promised to help us understand You better through its stories and words. I want to learn more about You and how I can please You. If there is something in the Bible that I don't understand, remind me that I can ask someone to help me. Best of all, I can ask You! Thank You, God. Amen.

––––––––––– **Think about it!** –––––––––––

What is your favorite Bible story and why?

The Bible Will Lead Me

*Your Word is a lamp to my
feet and a light to my path.*
PSALM 119:105

Dear God, You said that the Bible is like a lamp. When I
can't decide what to do, the Bible's words will help me to
see—like a light does in the darkness. As I learn more about
what is in the Bible, then I will know what to do when a
problem comes my way. Will You help me with that, Father?
I want the Bible to be like a bright light that leads me. Amen.

_____ **Think about it!** _____

How can you shine your light for Jesus in the world?

The Bible Makes Me Strong

Give me strength because of Your Word.
PSALM 119:28

Dear God, many of the Bible's stories are about people counting on You when they are troubled. I want to know and remember those stories. Everybody gets worried sometimes. When I do, I know that I can count on You and Your words in the Bible to help me. God, please speak to me through the Bible. Give me some words to remember—words that will help me to be strong whenever anything troubles me. Amen.

Think about it!

What helps you most when you are worried?

The Bible Teaches Me to Be Careful

And by them Your servant is told to be careful.
In obeying them there is great reward.
PSALM 19:11

Dear God, being careful is important because it helps keep me safe. My parents' and teachers' rules help me to stay out of trouble. Your words in the Bible help me to do that too. When I learn to obey Your rules, I can carefully choose right from wrong, and that helps keep me safe. Thank You, God, for giving us rules. I want to learn them and do my best to obey them. Amen.

—————————— **Think about it!** ——————————

How can God's Word help to keep you safe?

The Bible Helps Me to Grow as a Christian

Think about all this. Work at it so everyone may see you are growing as a Christian.
1 TIMOTHY 4:15

Dear God, You said that I will grow as a Christian if I practice what I learn from You. I want to learn something from the Bible every day. Will You remind me to do that? Please lead me to people who will read the Bible to me and guide me to understand its words. Teach me to memorize Bible verses that I can remember and store in my heart. I love You, God. Amen.

Think about it!

What's one thing you've learned from God's Word?

The Bible Is Forever

*"Heaven and earth will pass away,
but My words will not pass away."*
MATTHEW 24:35

Dear God, I know that *forever* means "always." You were not born or made by someone. You are God—You have always existed, and You will exist forever. Every word in the Bible is from You, and every word is true. You promise that what is in the Bible will not change. Your words are always and forever. Thank You for that. I know that I can count on the Bible every day of my life. Amen.

———————— **Think about it!** ————————

How often should you read the Bible?

God's Words Are Priceless

*The Law of Your mouth is better to me
than thousands of gold and silver pieces.*
PSALM 119:72

Dear God, when I imagine thousands of gold and silver coins I think, *That's a lot of money!* The Bible teaches that Your words are worth more than all the money in the world. Your words in the Bible are better than anything money can buy. It makes me happy knowing that You speak to me through the Bible. You must think that I'm special to give me such a valuable gift. I love You, God. Amen.

——— **Think about it!** ———

Why is God's Word better than money?

FAMILY, FRIENDS, AND NEIGHBORS

God Provides a Home for Me

God makes a home for those who are alone.
PSALM 68:6

Dear God, thank You for giving me a home, and thank You for my family. There are some people who are lonely and homeless tonight. But You promised to make a home for everyone. Will You remind all the lonely and homeless people that You love them? I believe that You have a special place somewhere ready and waiting for them. Lead them there, please. Put them in a family who loves You. Amen.

—————— **Think about it!** ——————

What is your favorite thing about home?

God Is Pleased When I Obey My Parents

Children, obey your parents in everything.
The Lord is pleased when you do.
COLOSSIANS 3:20

Dear heavenly Father, I know that You forgive me when I mess up and don't obey my parents. They forgive me too. I want to get better at obeying and following their rules. Will You help me with that? Help me to listen to their words and do what they say. Remind me that my parents are Your helpers. When I obey them, it pleases You, and that makes all of us happy. Thank You, God. Amen.

———— **Think about it!** ————

Is it sometimes hard to obey your
mom or dad? Why or why not?

God Helps Brothers and Sisters to Get Along

*See, how good and how pleasing it
is for brothers to live together as one!*
PSALM 133:1

Dear God, it makes You happy when brothers and sisters get along. You want us to love and help each other and share our toys. You expect us to be kind to one another and speak gently. It's hard for sisters and brothers to get along all the time! But, God, we have You to help us. Remind us of Your words, and help us to act in ways that are pleasing to You. Amen.

———————— **Think about it!** ————————

How does God want you to treat
your family members?

God Teaches Families to Stick Together

"Every city or family divided into groups that fight each other will not stand."
MATTHEW 12:25

Dear God, some families don't live together in the same house. Sometimes moms, dads, sisters, and brothers live apart. Still, You want them to love one another and keep on being a family. You are the One who holds families together with Your love. Help our family to count on You, and help us to count on each other. And remind us to pray for one another all the time. Good night, God. Amen.

——————— **Think about it!** ———————

Why is it important to pray
for your family members?

God Helps Us to Be Peaceful at Home

May there be peace within your walls.
May all go well within your houses.
PSALM 122:7

Dear God, our house is noisy sometimes when we play together and get along. I think our happy noise must make You smile. Father, I want all of our noise to be happy. Help us never to shout at one another or argue. I know that You want us to live in peace all the time. We need Your help to do that. Please give us a happy and peaceful home. Amen.

—————— **Think about it!** ——————

What kinds of noises are "happy" noises?

God Is Pleased When I
Share Him with Others

"Go home to your own people. Tell them
what great things the Lord has done for you."
MARK 5:19

Dear God, are there people in my family who don't know You? I want to tell them about You. I want to tell them all about the wonderful things that You do, and I want them to know that You love them. I especially want them to know about Your Son, Jesus, and that He is our way to heaven. Teach me to be Your helper, God. Show me how to lead others to You. Amen.

———————— **Think about it!** ————————

Who do you know that needs Jesus in their lives?

God Helps Me to Make Friends

He who stays away from others cares only about himself. He argues against all good wisdom.
PROVERBS 18:1

Dear God, thank You for friends. I want to have lots of friends so I can share You with them. I want to welcome new friends into my life all the time. Jesus is a friend to everyone. I want to be like Him. Maybe there is a kid in my neighborhood or at school who needs a friend. Will You get us together, God? Teach me to make friends and to be a good friend. Amen.

———————— **Think about it!** ————————

Who are your very best friends and why?

God Teaches Me to Love My Friends

A friend loves at all times.
Proverbs 17:17

Dear God, being a good friend takes practice. I believe that You want me to be a friend to everyone and to love them all the time. Jesus was that kind of friend. He loved people who were difficult to love. He prayed for them and wanted to help them. I want to be like Jesus. Help me to be patient with my friends, to love them and to forgive them if they misbehave. Amen.

----------- **Think about it!** -----------

In what ways can you show love to your friends?

God Helps Me to Encourage My Friends

*"Kindness from a friend should be
shown to a man without hope."*
JOB 6:14

Dear God, I want my friends to know that they are special.
I can do that through my words. If a friend is sad, will You
give me just the right words to cheer him up? Please give
me words to tell my friends that they did a good job or to
give them hope when they have something difficult to do.
And, God, remind me always to say kind things about my
friends. Amen.

Think about it!

In what ways can you encourage your friends?

God Teaches Me to Choose
My Friends Wisely

Do not let anyone fool you. Bad people can make
those who want to live good become bad.
1 CORINTHIANS 15:33

Dear God, You want me to be kind to everyone, but You also want me to choose my friends wisely. My job as a friend is to lead others to You. I need to be careful that a friend doesn't lead me away from You instead. Help me to be a good friend to everyone. Remind me that You are my best friend. I should always obey You and do what is right. Amen.

——————— **Think about it!** ———————

What does it mean to choose your friends wisely?

God Teaches Me to Get Along with My Neighbors

Each of us should live to please his neighbor.
This will help him grow in faith.
ROMANS 15:2

Dear God, when I think of neighbors, I think of the people next door, across the street, and on my block. Your idea of neighbors is bigger. To You, all the people in the world are neighbors. You want people everywhere to live as good neighbors, to be peaceful and kind to one another. Tonight, God, I pray for everyone in the world. Help us all to live like good neighbors and get along. Amen.

--- **Think about it!** ---

Who are your neighbors?

God Teaches Me to Love Others

God has taught you to love each other.
1 THESSALONIANS 4:9

Dear God, You love me all the time. I want to love people like You do. You have promised to teach me how to love others. So help me, please, to learn from You and from the Bible how to be more loving. Jesus is my very best teacher. As I learn more about Him, I know that I will learn how to love my friends and my enemies. Teach me, dear God. Thank You. Amen.

—————— **Think about it!** ——————

Is it really possible to love your enemies?

God Saves Me from My Enemies

I call to the Lord, Who has the right to be praised.
And I am saved from those who hate me.

PSALM 18:3

Dear God, there are some people who just don't want to be friends. If that hurts my feelings, remind me that I am worth being a friend. After all, Jesus chose me to be His—and that makes me feel special. Father, show me how to pray for anyone who doesn't want to be my friend. I know that You are their best friend. So please teach them to be loving and kind. Amen.

──────────── **Think about it!** ────────────

How can you be a good example of kindness and love?

God Helps My Love to Grow Stronger

*May the Lord make you grow in love for each other
and for everyone. We have this kind of love for you.*
1 THESSALONIANS 3:12

Dear God, You promise to help grow my love for others. I
know that You can help me to love everyone all the time,
even when they aren't very lovable. Your love for me is like
a warm, gentle hug that goes on forever. Will You grow my
love so it becomes gentle, big, and strong—the way that
You love me? I want to love others like You do, especially
when it is hard. Amen.

——————— **Think about it!** ———————

Do you need God to help you grow
your love for someone today?

God Teaches Me Not to Judge

"Do not say what is wrong in other people's lives. Then other people will not say what is wrong in your life."
MATTHEW 7:1

Dear God, a judge is someone who decides what is wrong in a person's life and how to fix it. Judging someone is Your job, not mine. I know that You want me to see the good in people and to leave it to You to decide what is wrong and how to fix it. Heavenly Father, open up my eyes and my heart to see the good in everyone and not to judge them. Amen.

Think about it!

Why is it important not to judge others?

God Teaches Me to Care about the Feelings of Others

Be happy with those who are happy.
Be sad with those who are sad.
ROMANS 12:15

Dear God, You always care about my feelings. You are happy when I am happy, and when I am unhappy or sick, You comfort me. You want me to care about others the way that You care about me. Teach me to be aware of how others feel and to care about their feelings. Show me how to celebrate with them when they are happy and help them when they are sad. Good night, God. Amen.

—————— **Think about it!** ——————

How can you show others
that you care about their feelings?

God Gives Me Good Role Models

Look at the man without blame.
And watch the man who is right and good.
PSALM 37:37

Dear God, tonight I ask You to bring good role models into my life—people who will teach me to live in ways that please You. Lead me to teachers, family members, and friends who will help me to learn more about You and the Bible. I want to grow up to behave in ways that are right and good. I know that is what You want for me too. Thank You, God. Amen.

──────────── **Think about it!** ────────────

Do you have any good role models in your life?

God Helps Me to Be a Good Example for Others

Let no one show little respect for you because you are young. Show other Christians how to live by your life. They should be able to follow you in the way you talk and in what you do. Show them how to live in faith and in love and in holy living.
1 Timothy 4:12

Dear God, I may be little, but that doesn't mean that I can't be a good role model for others. Please help me to show everyone I meet what it means to be well behaved. I can be kind, talk respectfully, and act in ways that are right and good. When others see how I behave, I hope that they will want to be like me—a kid who loves Jesus and tries hard to please Him. Amen.

--- **Think about it!** ---

Can kids really make a difference
in the world? If so, in what ways?

God Is Pleased When I Share

"Give to any person who asks you for something. Do not say no to the man who wants to use something of yours."
MATTHEW 5:42

Dear God, Jesus said a lot about sharing. He taught that we should always be willing to share what we have. Jesus shows me that sharing means more than just letting someone play with my toys. It means giving people my time and attention too—like Jesus did. I want to learn more about sharing. Will You teach me? Remind me not to be selfish. Teach me to care about the needs of others. Amen.

—————— **Think about it!** ——————

Is it hard for you to share? Why or why not?

God Rewards Me for Being Generous

"Give, and it will be given to you. You will have more than enough. It can be pushed down and shaken together and it will still run over as it is given to you. The way you give to others is the way you will receive in return."

LUKE 6:38

Dear God, I like Your promise about giving. You said that if I give good things to others, then You will give me good things in return. I can give by sharing and being kind, by saying nice things about others, and by caring about the feelings of others. Show me other ways to give, Father. Teach me to be generous with my giving. Help me to remember that giving is more important than getting. Thank You, God. Amen.

Think about it!

What does it mean to be generous?

God Teaches Me How to Treat Others

*"Do for other people what you
would like to have them do for you."*
Luke 6:31

Dear God, You put important rules in the Bible for me to learn. One of them says that I should do for other people what I would like them to do for me. Please help me to remember that rule. Even if someone treats me badly, remind me to treat that person the way that I would like to be treated. Your rules are always good, Father. They teach me the right way to live. Amen.

——————— **Think about it!** ———————

How would God like us to treat others?

God Loves a Joyful Giver

*God loves a man who gives
because he wants to give.*
2 CORINTHIANS 9:7

Dear God, I am learning that giving is fun. When I willingly give my help to someone who needs it or when I draw a picture or make a little gift for someone, I often get smiles and hugs in return. That makes me happy! The Bible says that You love it when people give because they want to. Thank You for teaching me to give unselfishly, and thanks for the smiles and hugs too. Amen.

—————— **Think about it!** ——————

What does it mean to give unselfishly?

God Is Pleased When I Use Good Language

Watch your talk! No bad words should be coming from your mouth. Say what is good. Your words should help others grow as Christians.
EPHESIANS 4:29

Dear God, when I hear bad words, You remind me not to repeat them. You want me to always say what is good. Jesus used His words to set a good example and lead others to You. God, will You help me to be that kind of example for others? I want all the words from my mouth to be good. Amen.

—————— **Think about it!** ——————

Why is it important to choose
your words carefully?

God Helps Me to Be Kind

*"You must have loving-kindness just
as your Father has loving-kindness."*
LUKE 6:36

Dear God, before I sleep tonight, I will think of some ways that You show kindness to me. You go wherever I go, watch over me, and keep me safe. You give me people who love me and take care of me. You forgive me when I mess up and teach me to be good. Please help me to think of a long list of Your kindnesses, and remind me to be kind to everyone too. Amen.

——————— **Think about it!** ———————

In what ways does God show
you kindness every day?

God Helps Me to Comfort Others

He gives us comfort in all our troubles. Then we can comfort other people who have the same troubles. We give the same kind of comfort God gives us.
2 Corinthians 1:4

Dear God, I may be young, but still I can be Your helper. One thing I can do is comfort people and cheer them up when they need it. I can be like those who help me feel better when I am sick or sad. Soft words, a gentle hug, and even a happy song can help comfort someone and make that person feel better. Teach me to be a good comforter, God. I love You. Amen.

--- **Think about it!** ---

In what ways are you God's helper?

GOD AND ME

God Loves Me

*I pray that you will be able to understand
how wide and how long and how
high and how deep His love is.*
EPHESIANS 3:18

Dear God, will You help me to understand how big Your love is? The Bible says that Your love for me is greater than any other love. There are people here on earth who love me with all of their hearts. But You love me even more! Your love for me is higher than the sky and deeper than the ocean. It makes me feel special that You love me so much. I love You too. Amen.

—— **Think about it!** ——

Does God love you more than
anyone else on earth does?

Nothing Can Separate Me from God's Love

For I know that nothing can keep us from the love of God. Death cannot! Life cannot! Angels cannot! Leaders cannot! Any other power cannot! Hard things now or in the future cannot!

ROMANS 8:38

Dear God, if I don't feel Your love all around me, please remind me that it is still there. You rule heaven and earth, and You promised that nothing can separate me from Your love. No one is more powerful than You. You are the great King of everything, and no one can take Your love away from me. When I close my eyes to sleep tonight, please wrap me warm in Your love. Amen.

Think about it!

Can anything get in the way
of God's amazing love?

I Can't See God, but He Is There

"God is Spirit. Those who worship Him must worship Him in spirit and in truth."
JOHN 4:24

Dear God, I wish that I could see You. But since I can't, I just have to believe that You are here. Believing in You is a big part of trusting You. You want me to believe in You without seeing You with my own two eyes. I can do that, God! I can believe without seeing. I know in my heart that You are always here watching over me all the time. Amen.

—————— **Think about it!** ——————

How do you know God is there
if you can't see Him?

God Sees Me

The eyes of the Lord are on those who do what is right and good. His ears are open to their cry.
PSALM 34:15

Dear Father, I can't see You, but You see me. You especially like seeing when I do things that are right and good. And when I need Your help, You see that too. Thank You for keeping Your eyes on me, God. Wherever I go and whatever I do, I know that You see me. You hear my prayers, and You know exactly what I need. I will never be alone, because You are with me. Amen.

—————————— **Think about it!** ——————————

Are you ever really alone? Why or why not?

God Can Fix What Is Wrong

"Do not be afraid, just believe."
MARK 5:36

Dear God, when I am worried or afraid, I sometimes forget about You. The things I worry about fill up my head, and I forget that You are with me. I need Your help with that. Teach me to pray when something is bothering me. Help me to believe with all my heart that You can fix whatever is wrong. Remind me to keep my thoughts set on You. Thank You, God. Amen.

Think about it!

When you are distracted by bothersome thoughts, why is it important to focus on God?

God Helps Grow My Love for Him

*"And you must love the Lord your
God with all your heart and with all
your soul and with all your strength."*
DEUTERONOMY 6:5

Dear God, You want my love for You to be stronger than the love I have for anyone or anything else. That is how I want to love You. Will You help my love grow? Remind me to think about You all the time and to notice the good things You do for me. Fill up my heart with love for You, and teach me to share that love with others. Good night, God. Amen.

———— **Think about it!** ————

How much do you love God?
And why do you love Him?

God Teaches Me to Obey Him

"Follow the Lord your God and fear Him.
Keep His Laws, and listen to His voice.
Work for Him, and hold on to Him."
Deuteronomy 13:4

Dear God, the Bible teaches me to listen to Your words and follow Your rules. If I forget to do that, please forgive me. Teach me the ways that You want me to live. Then help me to put what I learn into action. I want to please You, God. I want to learn from You, listen to You, and obey You. I want to follow Your ways. Help me to do my best. Amen.

─────── **Think about it!** ───────

How can you know that your
behavior is pleasing to God?

God's Plans Are Better Than Mine

*The mind of a man plans his way,
but the Lord shows him what to do.*
PROVERBS 16:9

Dear God, sometimes my plans don't work out the way that I want them to. When that happens, I have to remember that Your plans are greater than mine. You know exactly what I should be doing. If I trust You, You will show me what to do. When my plans don't work out and I can't understand why, remind me that You have a better plan. I know I can count on it. Amen.

——————————— **Think about it!** ———————————

Is God's plan *always* better than your plan?

God Is Always Working on Me

*I am sure that God Who began the good
work in you will keep on working in you
until the day Jesus Christ comes again.*
PHILIPPIANS 1:6

Dear God, when You created me, that was just the beginning of Your plan for me. Every day, You are working on me, helping me to become the best that I can be. Even when I am old, You will still be helping me to become more like You. I am grateful that You love me so much and that You just keep making me better and better. Thank You, God! Good night. Amen.

—————— **Think about it!** ——————

Is it important to always give God your very best?

God Helps Me to Trust Him in All That I Do

Trust your work to the Lord,
and your plans will work out well.
PROVERBS 16:3

Dear God, I believe that You will help me with everything I do. You promise that if I trust my work to You, my plans will work out well. Father, before I start any project, remind me to say a little prayer and ask for Your help. Remind me that You'll work on that project with me. I know that I'll do a great job with You as my helper. I love You, God. Amen.

————————— **Think about it!** —————————

Do you often pray and ask God for His help?

Jesus Is My Role Model

*Do as God would do. Much-loved
children want to do as their fathers do.*
Ephesians 5:1

Dear heavenly Father, when I don't know what to do or say or how to act, I know Who can show me—Jesus! The Bible is filled with examples of how Jesus behaved. Jesus always knew the right things to do. The more that I learn about Him, the better I will understand how to act in any situation. I want Jesus to be my role model. Will You help me to learn more about Him? Amen.

—————— **Think about it!** ——————

If you're confused, who—or what—
can help you to do the right thing?

God Has a Purpose for Me

He is working in you. God is helping you obey Him.
God is doing what He wants done in you.
PHILIPPIANS 2:13

Dear God, I believe that You have a good plan for me and a purpose for my life. I wonder what Your plan for me is. I trust that You are working out that plan right now in ways that I can't see. As I grow and become older, will You show me more of Your plan? I want to be Your helper. Help me to obey You and follow wherever You lead me. Amen.

———————— **Think about it!** ————————

Do you have any worries about the future?

God Will Use Me to Do Good

But the Lord said to me, "Do not say, 'I am only a boy.' You must go everywhere I send you. And you must say whatever I tell you. Do not be afraid of them. For I am with you to take you out of trouble," says the Lord.
JEREMIAH 1:7–8

Dear God, You love children, and You said that although we are young, kids can be Your helpers. How can I help You, God? I know that I can help by telling my friends and family about You. I can help by behaving well and being a good example. What are some other ways that I can help You? Please show me. Teach me how to spread Your goodness around wherever I go. Amen.

——————— **Think about it!** ———————

In what ways can you spread
God's goodness wherever you go?

God Is My Safe Place

God is our safe place and our strength.
He is always our help when we are in trouble.
PSALM 46:1

Dear God, You promised to be my safe place and strength. I like that promise! Wherever I go and whatever I do, I know that I am safe because You are with me. You promised to always help me when trouble comes along. You are stronger than anything, so I know that You have power over whatever bothers me. Thank You, God, for being my safe place. Thank You for helping me all the time. Amen.

Think about it!

When trouble comes along,
what do you usually do?

God Is with Me Wherever I Go

"Have I not told you? Be strong and have strength of heart! Do not be afraid or lose faith. For the Lord your God is with you anywhere you go."
JOSHUA 1:9

Dear God, You said that You want me to be strong in my heart. That means You want me to believe with all my heart that You will keep Your promises. I believe that, God! You said that You are with me anywhere I go, and I believe that too. When I am afraid or if I forget that You are with me, remind me. Fill up my heart with trust in You. Amen.

—————— **Think about it!** ——————

How does it feel to know that
God is *always* with you?

God Holds My Hand

*"For I am the Lord your God Who holds
your right hand, and Who says to you,
'Do not be afraid. I will help you.' "*
ISAIAH 41:13

Dear God, You say in the Bible that You hold my right hand.
I can't feel Your hand holding mine, but if You said it, then
it is true. The Bible says that You hold my hand and say, "Do
not be afraid. I will help you." I want to remember that, God.
Even if I can't feel it, I want to believe that everywhere I go
we are together, with You holding my hand. Amen.

—————————— **Think about it!** ——————————

What things are you afraid of?
And how can you get rid of those fears?

God Tells Angels to Watch Over Me

*For He will tell His angels to care for
you and keep you in all your ways.*
PSALM 91:11

Dear Father, I believe in angels. You promised to tell them to watch over me and take care of me. That is a good promise to remember when I lie down to sleep. When I close my eyes, I know that You will watch over me, and Your angels will too. Thank You, God, for watching over me tonight, and thank You for Your angels. I will sleep safe and sound knowing that they are with me. Amen.

—————————— **Think about it!** ——————————

Do you think it's easier to sleep knowing God and His angels are always watching over you? Why or why not?

God Protects Me

He will cover you with His wings. And under His wings you will be safe. He is faithful like a safe-covering and a strong wall.

PSALM 91:4

Dear God, the words in the Bible help me to imagine how much You care for me. The Bible says that You protect me like an angel, covering me with Your wings, keeping me safe all the time. It says that You are like a strong wall that protects me. Teach me, Father, to always count on You to protect me. Keep that picture in my head of an angel covering me with its wings. Amen.

―――――――――――― **Think about it!** ――――――――――――

How does God protect you?

God Is with Me When I Feel Sad

The Lord is near to those who have a broken heart.
And He saves those who are broken in spirit.
PSALM 34:18

Dear God, when I am sad and I cry, I need to remember that You promise to be near me and help me to feel happy again. When I am sad, the first thing I should do is pray and talk to You. Will You remind me to do that? I know that You want to hear about my troubles. I believe that You want to make my sadness go away. Thank You, God. I love You. Amen.

Think about it!

Can God really help take away
your sadness? Why or why not?

God Is with Me When I Get Hurt

" 'For I will heal you. I will heal you
where you have been hurt,' says the Lord."
JEREMIAH 30:17

Dear God, when I get hurt, Your love is like a big bandage. You will heal my hurt. I can count on that, because You promised. If I have a little hurt, You will help it go away. If I have a big hurt that needs a doctor, You will help me to be strong and brave. You and the doctor will take care of me. Thank You, God, for healing my hurts. Amen.

Think about it!

In what ways can God heal you?

God Takes Care of Me When I Am Afraid

*"So do not be afraid. I will take
care of you and your little ones."*
GENESIS 50:21

Dear God, You tell everyone not to be afraid, and You promise moms and dads that You will take care of their little ones. I forget sometimes that You are the heavenly Father to grown-ups too. They count on You for help to care for themselves and their families. Thank You for taking such good care of our family. Remind us that with You in charge, we never have to feel afraid. Amen.

--- **Think about it!** ---

Do grown-ups ever get afraid too? If so,
who can help them with their fears?

God Will Take My Worries Away

Give all your worries to Him
because He cares for you.
1 PETER 5:7

Dear God, I worry sometimes. I worry when I have to do something new or when I feel unsure about what to do or about how something will work out. I need to remember that You are my best friend and helper. You care so much for me that You want to take my worries away. Thank You! Please take all my worries. I will count on You to work everything out because You love me. Amen.

--------- **Think about it!** ---------

Can you truly count on God to help
you control your worries?

God Will Help Me to Listen

The way of a fool is right in his own eyes,
but a wise man listens to good teaching.
PROVERBS 12:15

Dear heavenly Father, will You help me to become a better listener? I believe that listening will help me to learn. When I listen to my parents, I learn to behave. Listening to teachers helps me to learn about the world. Best of all, when I listen to Your words, I learn to be a better Christian. Please help me to pay attention when people are talking to me. I want their words to teach me. Amen.

--- **Think about it!** ---

What qualities make a good listener?

God Will Help Me to Learn

A wise man will hear and grow in learning.
A man of understanding will become able
to understand a saying and a picture-story,
the words of the wise and what they mean.
PROVERBS 1:5–6

Dear God, I know that learning is important. You want me to listen and learn so I will grow up to be wise. Will You help me to learn? I want to learn all about the world and how to do things. I want to listen to my teachers and ask questions. And if there is something that I don't understand, God, please don't let me get discouraged. Just help me to understand. Amen.

────────── **Think about it!** ──────────

What is your favorite thing to learn about?

God Will Help Me to Keep on Learning

*Give teaching to a wise man and he will
be even wiser. Teach a man who is right
and good, and he will grow in learning.*
PROVERBS 9:9

Dear God, learning goes on forever. The more I learn, the
wiser I will be. I want to keep on learning about You. I want
to read the Bible every day and discover all of Your promises.
I want to help others to learn about You too. I won't stop
learning! Thank You for giving me a mind that can learn.
Help me to keep on learning every day of my life. Amen.

--- **Think about it!** ---

Do you ever really stop learning?

God Helps Me to Have Faith
When I Don't Understand

*Through faith we understand that the world
was made by the Word of God. Things we see
were made from what could not be seen.*

HEBREWS 11:3

Dear God, if I get discouraged because I don't understand something, remind me that You will help me. Build up my faith in You. Faith means trusting that You are always with me and You will help me all the time. You made everything, and You understand everything. When learning is hard, I will trust You to help me. I will ask for help from my teachers and also from You. Thank You, God. Amen.

──────── **Think about it!** ────────

What is your most difficult subject
in school? Can God help you with that?

God Helps Me to Be Patient

Wait for the Lord. Be strong. Let your heart be strong. Yes, wait for the Lord.
PSALM 27:14

Dear God, sometimes when things are hard, I want to give up. When that happens, I promise to say a prayer and ask You to help me. Talking to You always makes me feel better. I don't want to give up, God, and I know that You don't want me to give up either. Patience is an important part of learning. Please give me the strength to be patient and not get discouraged. Amen.

--- **Think about it!** ---

Have you ever felt like giving up? When?

God Cares about What I Watch

I will set no sinful thing in front of my eyes. I hate the work of those who are not faithful. It will not get hold of me.
PSALM 101:3

Dear heavenly Father, You know everything about me, even what I like to watch. You know all about what is on television and in video games. You care about what I see. Please help me to make wise choices. Teach me what is right and good for me to see, and keep me away from the rest. I want to remember that whatever I watch, You are watching too. I love You, God. Amen.

—————————— **Think about it!** ——————————

What is your favorite movie or TV show?

God Cares about What I Think

Christian brothers, keep your minds thinking about whatever is true, whatever is respected, whatever is right, whatever is pure, whatever can be loved, and whatever is well thought of. If there is anything good and worth giving thanks for, think about these things.
PHILIPPIANS 4:8

Dear God, You care about what I think. You know all my thoughts all the time. I want my thoughts to be respectful and pure. I will set my mind on the right things to do. I will think about You, and I will be thankful because You are so good to me. Please fill up my mind with good thoughts, God. I want everything I think about to please You. Thank You. Amen.

Think about it!

Why does God care about your thoughts?

God Honors My Quietness

Do your best to live a quiet life.
Learn to do your own work well.
1 THESSALONIANS 4:11

Dear Father in heaven, my friends and I are noisy when we play. I think You enjoy seeing us happy and laughing together. But sometimes it is important to be quiet. I need quiet time every day to talk with You and listen to Your words. Help me to make a special time every day to be alone with You. I will use the time before I sleep to pray and think about You. Good night, God. Amen.

—————————— **Think about it!** ——————————

Why is it important to be quiet sometimes?

Going to Church Will Make Me Happy

How happy are those who live in Your house!
They are always giving thanks to You.
PSALM 84:4

Dear God, You said that going to church will make people happy. A church is Your house here on earth. You open up the doors and welcome everyone inside. We learn all about You in church. We pray together, sing, and thank You for being our God. Church is where Sunday school is—where kids have fun learning about You. Thank You, God, for churches. Thank You for inviting me into Your house. Amen.

——————— **Think about it!** ———————

What do you love most about your church?

God Is Pleased When I Praise Him

Praise the Lord! For it is good to sing praises to our God. For it is pleasing and praise is right.
PSALM 147:1

Dear God, thank You for giving me a voice to sing with. It pleases You when people sing to praise You. You hear every song we sing. I want my songs to thank You for being so wonderful. I want to sing about the Bible and the stories that I've learned about You and Jesus. My songs will tell You how much I love You. Will You help me to learn some new songs too? Amen.

——————— **Think about it!** ———————

Are there other ways to praise
God than with singing?

God Will Be Pleased by My Good Words and Thoughts

Let the words of my mouth and the thoughts of my heart be pleasing in Your eyes, O Lord, my Rock and the One Who saves me.

PSALM 19:14

Dear God, I want all my words and thoughts to please You. Will You help me with that? I know I will mess up sometimes and say and think things that won't make You happy. But I know that You will forgive me and help me to do better. One of the reasons that I love You is because You always love me and forgive me even when I mess up. Thank You, God! Amen.

Think about it!

If you mess up, what should you do?

God Will Make Me Happy When I Do What Is Right

*You meet him who finds joy
in doing what is right and good,
who remembers You in Your ways.*
ISAIAH 64:5

Dear God, thank You for filling me up with glad feelings. When I do what is right, I feel peaceful in my heart, and when I do what is good, I feel happy. You are the One who teaches me how to be right and good. As I learn from You and try my best to be like You, I feel close to You, and that is the best feeling of all. Good night, God. Amen.

— **Think about it!** —

When do you feel closest to God?

God Will Help Me to Do What Is Good

*Remember to do good and help
each other. Gifts like this please God.*
Hebrews 13:16

Dear God, I know that You are pleased when people are good and helpful. I want to please You, so will You teach me how to spread Your love all around? Show me all kinds of ways to do good things and be helpful to my family, friends, and community. Make me Your helper. Lead me to the people who need my help, and show me how to help them. Thank You, God. Amen.

——— **Think about it!** ———

How can you shine God's light into your community?

God Will Lead Me to Work for Peace

Work for the things that make peace and help each other become stronger Christians.
ROMANS 14:19

Dear God, the world needs You. It needs the kind of peace that only You can give it. I want to help You to bring more peace into the world. I can do that by sharing what I know about You with others. If everyone learns to trust in You and Your Son, Jesus, the world will become a more peaceful place. Help me to be a peacemaker at home, at school, and everywhere I go. Amen.

—————————— **Think about it!** ——————————

Why does the world need God?

I Can Do Great Things with God's Help

*God is able to do much more than we ask
or think through His power working in us.*
EPHESIANS 3:20

Dear God, I wonder what I will be when I grow up. You promised that I can do much more than I think I can because Your power is at work inside me. Lead me to give my best to everything I do. Remind me that You have a great plan for my future. I will always be Your helper here on earth. Teach me, and help me to learn so we can do great things together! Amen.

——————— **Think about it!** ———————

Why is it important to always give
your best effort in everything you do?

God's Spirit Gives Me Good Gifts

*But the fruit that comes from having the Holy
Spirit in our lives is: love, joy, peace, not giving up,
being kind, being good, having faith, being gentle,
and being the boss over our own desires.*
GALATIANS 5:22–23

Dear God, good gifts come from You living inside my heart.
You give me good feelings like love, joy, and peace. You
help me to behave in ways that set a good example and to
never give up. You teach me to have faith and to be kind and
gentle toward others. When I have to choose between right
and wrong, You help me to make the best choice. Thank You,
God, for these good gifts. Amen.

—————————— **Think about it!** ——————————

Where do all good gifts come from?

No One Is Perfect Except God

For all men have sinned and have
missed the shining-greatness of God.
ROMANS 3:23

Dear God, You are the only One Who is perfect. Humans make mistakes all the time. But when we mess up, You promise to forgive us when we trust Jesus. If I believe in Jesus and ask Him into my heart, I can tell Him what I've done wrong—and He will forgive me, always and forever! Remind me, God, that Jesus is my best friend, and He will help me to obey You. Amen.

Think about it!

Why is it important to talk to
God about your mistakes?

God Will Test Me

My Christian brothers, you should be happy when you have all kinds of tests. You know these prove your faith. It helps you not to give up.
JAMES 1:2–3

Dear God, You are my teacher, and teachers sometimes give tests. You will test me by asking me to be patient when waiting is hard or by saying no to something that I want. I can pass Your tests by continuing to love and trust You, especially when I don't understand. Your tests help me to learn and be strong. When You test me, God, please help me to keep on believing in and trusting You. Amen.

—————— **Think about it!** ——————

How can you show God that you trust Him?

God Will Do Something New

"Do not remember the things that have happened before. Do not think about the things of the past. See, I will do a new thing. It will begin happening now. Will you not know about it? I will even make a road in the wilderness, and rivers in the desert."

Isaiah 43:18–19

Dear God, You do such wonderful things! I wonder what new things You have planned. Remind me to keep my eyes open to watch for Your good works. Every day, I will look for something new, and when I find it I will thank You for it. I will make a list of the new things I see. Help me to make a long list, God. Your work is all around me. I love You. Amen.

—————————— **Think about it!** ——————————

What wonderful thing did God do today?

God Has a Place for Me in Heaven

"Do not be afraid, little flock. Your Father wants to give you the holy nation of God."
LUKE 12:32

Dear God, living on earth is nice, but You have an even better place waiting for me—heaven! Heaven is Your kingdom. It is a beautiful and perfect place where everyone is happy all the time. You want to share heaven with me always and forever. Thank You for that, God. It might be a very long time before I get there, but I will look forward to living with You in heaven someday. Amen.

—————— **Think about it!** ——————

What do you think it will be like to live in heaven?

I Am God's Forever

This is God, our God forever and ever.
He will show us the way until death.
PSALM 48:14

Dear God, You are my helper and my best friend. You are with me right now, and we will be together forever. You promised, and I believe You. I know You will always be my heavenly Father, and I will always be Your child. You must really love me to want us to be together forever! I love You too. Cuddle me up warm in Your love tonight, and give me happy dreams. Good night, God. Amen.

Think about it!

In what ways is God your helper and best friend?

DEAR GOD, I TRUST YOU

Trusting God Makes Me Strong

*Those who trust in the Lord are like Mount Zion,
which cannot be moved but stands forever.*
PSALM 125:1

Dear God, You promised that if I trust You, I can stand up to anything that gets in my way. You are the Father of all fathers. You have power over everything, and You always know the right thing to do. I know that I can trust You to help me all the time. So please build up my trust in You. Make it big and strong. Help me to trust You with everything I do. Amen.

Think about it!

Is it easy for you to stand up to things that get in the way of your relationship with God? Why or why not?

God Has Good Plans for Me

" 'For I know the plans I have for you,'
says the Lord, 'plans for well-being and not
for trouble, to give you a future and a hope.' "
JEREMIAH 29:11

Dear God, I wish that I knew what Your plans are for me. But for now, that is Your secret. You promise that Your plans for me are good. You want me to have a good life. That is all I can know right now about my future. I need to trust You with the rest. I do trust You, God. I believe that You have great things planned for me because You love me. Amen.

Think about it!

What plans do you think God
might have for your life?

God Will Always Help Me

*Let us go with complete trust to the throne of God.
We will receive His loving-kindness and have His
loving-favor to help us whenever we need it.*
HEBREWS 4:16

Dear God, sometimes I like to imagine You as the great King sitting on Your throne in heaven. You are the sort of king who welcomes people in. We can come to You at any time, night or day, to pray and ask for Your help. Best of all, we can trust You to listen to us and help us. God—I am so glad that You are my King! Thank You. I love You. Amen.

—————————— **Think about it!** ——————————

What kind of king is God?

God Leads Me

Trust in the Lord with all your heart, and do not trust in your own understanding. Agree with Him in all your ways, and He will make your paths straight.
PROVERBS 3:5–6

Dear God, when there are things that I don't understand and I am confused about what to do, I know that You will help me. Remind me, please, that You are my leader and I need to trust You. I need to remember everything that I have learned about You from the Bible and believe in Your promises. When I do that, You will help me to understand and show me the right thing to do. Amen.

—————— **Think about it!** ——————

Why is God such a great leader?

God Will Show Me the Way

*Teach me the way I should go
for I lift up my soul to You.*
PSALM 143:8

Dear God, I feel safe knowing that You are always with me. If I have to go someplace I have never been before, I don't have to worry because You know the way to get there. If I don't know how to do something, You know how to get it done. All I have to do is trust You to show me the way. Please teach me to trust You even more. Thank You, God. Amen.

—————————— **Think about it!** ——————————

How does God's Word show
you the right way to go?

God Will Give Me Everything I Need

*And my God will give you everything you need
because of His great riches in Christ Jesus.*
PHILIPPIANS 4:19

Dear heavenly Father, You promise to give me everything I need. But sometimes the things that I ask You for don't fit into Your plan for me. You know better than I do what I need. I might feel disappointed, but still I have to trust that You know best. Help me to understand that, please. Teach me to trust You all the time, even when You don't give me what I want. Amen.

— Think about it! —

Have you ever asked God for
something and He said "no"?

Jesus Will Give Me His Best

"Until now you have not asked for anything in My name. Ask and you will receive. Then your joy will be full."
JOHN 16:24

Dear Jesus, You are my friend, and I know that I can trust You. I can ask You for anything and trust that You will do Your best to help me. You know what God's plans are for me, and You will teach me what to ask for when I pray. I want what You know is best for me. So help me to put all my trust in You. I love You, Jesus! Amen.

—————————— **Think about it!** ——————————

Why is it important to trust
God's plan for your life?

Jesus Is Always near Me

*Come close to God and He
will come close to you.*
JAMES 4:8

Dear Jesus, when I put all my trust in You, I feel closer to You. It is like I am resting in Your arms, and You are rocking me to sleep. I feel safe and sound knowing that You are near to me. Help me to remember that You are always with me and that You love me. All I have to do is say Your name, Jesus, and know that You are here. Amen.

―――――――― **Think about it!** ――――――――

Do you trust God with all
your heart? Why or why not?

God Understands Me

O Lord, You have looked through me and have known me. You know when I sit down and when I get up. You understand my thoughts from far away.
<small>PSALM 139:1–2</small>

Dear God, I trust with all my heart that You understand me. You created me. You put me together and You called me Your child. You know all about me. You see when I sit down and when I get up and everything I do. You understand what I am thinking all the time, and because You understand me so well, I know that I can always trust You. Thank You, heavenly Father! I love You. Amen.

Think about it!

Does God know you better
than your own parents do?

God Gives Me Confidence

For the Lord will be your trust. He will
keep your foot from being caught.
PROVERBS 3:26

Dear God, when I have to do something new, I worry sometimes that I won't get it right. When that happens, I will believe in Your help. You promised me that I can trust You. I will remember that You are always with me. Will You give me the strength to try new things without being afraid? Teach me to be sure that I can do difficult things by putting all my faith in You. Amen.

—————— **Think about it!** ——————

What makes you feel brave?

God Gives Me Wisdom

If you do not have wisdom, ask God for it.
He is always ready to give it to you and will
never say you are wrong for asking.
JAMES 1:5

Dear God, You have taught me that wisdom means making good choices. That is what I want to do. I want to make decisions that please You because they are right. I know that I can trust You to lead me. You said that You want me to ask You for wisdom. So please give me the wisdom to do what is right. Remind me to pray and ask for Your help. Thank You, God. Amen.

―――――――――― **Think about it!** ――――――――――

What exactly is wisdom? And how do you get it?

God Gives Me Power over Sin

Every child of God has power over the sins of the world. The way we have power over the sins of the world is by our faith.
1 JOHN 5:4

Dear God, You said that all of Your children have power over sin. I know that sin means the bad things in the world. You give me power over those bad things by helping me to make right decisions. Heavenly Father, whenever sin gets in my way, will You remind me that You are my helper and protector? Please make my trust in You really strong so we can stand up to sin together. Amen.

————————— **Think about it!** —————————

How can you have power over sin?

God Helps Me to Obey Him

*"I will give you a new heart and
put a new spirit within you."*
EZEKIEL 36:26

Dear God, sin is all over the place, so sometimes it's hard to stay away from it. All humans mess up sometimes and give in to sin. But You promise to forgive us if we ask You to. You promise to clean all the sin out of our hearts. God, when I do something that I know is wrong, I promise to tell You about it. I trust that You will forgive me. Amen.

─────────── **Think about it!** ───────────

What is obedience?

God Helps Me to Do My Best

With God's help we will do well.
PSALM 60:12

Dear God, I worry sometimes that what I do might not be good enough. Please help me not to worry about that. Another of Your promises is that You will help me to do well. I know that I can trust You. So whenever I think that I might not be good at something, please give me the courage to try and to believe that You will help me to stay calm and do my best. Amen.

———————— **Think about it!** ————————

What should you do if you ever feel
like you're not good enough?

God Watches Over Me

*The Lord will watch over your
coming and going, now and forever.*
PSALM 121:8

Dear God, I believe that You are always watching over me. I believe with all my heart that You see everything I do. Whether I am going someplace or coming home, You see me. You watch over me wherever I am all the time, and You promise to watch over me forever. I love You so much, God. Thank You for being with me everywhere and taking such good care of me. Amen.

———— **Think about it!** ————

Does God *always* see you?

God Protects Me from Darkness

"I came to the world to be a Light. Anyone who puts his trust in Me will not be in darkness."
JOHN 12:46

Dear God, when You put the moon and stars in the sky, were You thinking about kids? The moon and stars are like night-lights. When I see them, I know that You are all around me. You sent Jesus into the world to be a light too. His love is like a light in the darkness. Help me to remember—when I put my trust in Him, I will never be alone in the dark. Amen.

─────────── **Think about it!** ───────────

Are you afraid of the dark?
Why or why not?

God Is with Me When I Sleep

I will lie down and sleep in peace.
O Lord, You alone keep me safe.
PSALM 4:8

Dear God, thank You for nighttime and rest. Thank You for my comfortable bed, my blankets, and good-night hugs and kisses. Thank You for listening to my bedtime prayers and for sending angels to watch over me. When I close my eyes to sleep, I will feel cozy and safe because You will be right here at my bedside, all night long. I feel sleepy now, God, so I will say good night. I love You. Amen.

———————— **Think about it!** ————————

Do you always talk to God at bedtime?

God Is with Me When I Wake Up

When I awake, I am still with You.
Psalm 139:18

Dear God, when I wake up tomorrow morning, You are the first One I will say good morning to. When I wake up, I trust that You will be with me, because You have been here all night long watching over me while I sleep. Tomorrow morning, I will thank You for staying with me all night. I will ask You to guide me through a new day. Good night, God. I will see You in the morning. Amen.

Think about it!

Do you always talk to God when
you wake up in the morning?

God Gives Me Joy

"You will go out with joy, and be led out in peace. The mountains and the hills will break out into sounds of joy before you. And all the trees of the field will clap their hands."
Isaiah 55:12

Dear God, thank You for happiness! You make me so happy when I laugh and play. Knowing You fills me up with joy. The Bible says that Your whole creation is happy because of You. It is almost like the mountains and hills sing to You and the trees clap their branches like hands. I love thinking about that, God. I love imagining everything in the world shouting, "Hooray, God! You are so amazing." Amen.

--- **Think about it!** ---

In what ways does God bring you joy?

God Gives Me Hope

Our hope comes from God.
Romans 15:13

Dear God, hope is wanting something that I don't have yet. I hope for many things. I hope for everyday things like sunshine, feeling happy, and having fun with my friends. I hope for big things too, like peace in the world and health for sick people. Will You help me to remember that hope comes from trusting in You? I trust that You will give me, and the whole world, whatever You know is best. Amen.

———————— **Think about it!** ————————

What exactly is hope? Where does it come from?

God Keeps Me Safe

*Even if I walk into trouble, You will keep my life safe.
You will put out Your hand against the anger of those
who hate me. And Your right hand will save me.*
PSALM 138:7

Dear heavenly Father, I feel so safe knowing that You are with me. You promise to keep my life safe. You promise to stand up to anyone who dislikes me or tries to hurt me. You will stand up to them even if I can't do it myself. My job is to trust You. I need to remember that You are the Father of all of us—and, always, You hold my hand. Amen.

—————— **Think about it!** ——————

What—or who—makes you feel safe?

God Helps When I Am in Trouble

"Call on Me in the day of trouble. I will take you out of trouble, and you will honor Me."
PSALM 50:15

Dear God, if I get into trouble for not doing what my parents say or for not following Your rules, I trust that You will help me. You promise that if I call out to You and ask for Your help, You will be there. Please teach me to do what is right so I won't get into trouble. But if I do get into trouble, remind me to pray and ask You to help me. Amen.

―――――――― **Think about it!** ――――――――

When you're in trouble, do you
say a prayer and ask God for help?

God Forgives Me

If we tell Him our sins, He is faithful and we can depend on Him to forgive us of our sins. He will make our lives clean from all sin.

1 JOHN 1:9

Dear God, sin is such a sneaky thing. It creeps up on me and leads me into trouble. When that happens, I know that I need to tell You about it right away. You won't be mad at me. I can trust You to forgive me and help me. Your love makes everything fresh and brand new. Thank You for always forgiving me, and thank You for helping me to do better next time. Amen.

--- **Think about it!** ---

When you mess up and ask God to forgive you, does He allow you to start over?

Jesus Takes My Sins Away

He has taken our sins from us as
far as the east is from the west.
PSALM 103:12

Dear Jesus, You are God's Son, and He sent You here to rule over sin. Sin is like the worst bully. It wants to lead everyone into doing wrong things. But, Jesus, You have power over sin. Sin is afraid of You! With You as my protector and friend, sin is afraid of me too. Help me to stay close to You, trust You, and do what is right so we can fight sin together. Amen.

—— **Think about it!** ——

How is sin like a bully?

God Helps When I Feel Unsure

For God did not give us a spirit of fear.
He gave us a spirit of power and
of love and of a good mind.
2 TIMOTHY 1:7

Dear God, the first time I have to do something, I might feel a little afraid. If that happens, I know that I can trust You to help me. You promise to give me power over those scared feelings. You gave me a good mind to make good choices. I know that You love me and You will help me to be brave when I feel unsure. Thank You for taking good care of me, God. Amen.

Think about it!

How can God help you have
power over your fears?

God Helps When I Don't Know What to Say

"I say to you, on the day men stand before God, they will have to give an answer for every word they have spoken that was not important."
MATTHEW 12:36

Dear God, I think You invented words to do good things. I want my words to please You. Bad words, angry words, and mean words make You unhappy. I want my words to praise You and make You proud of me. I want my words to make people feel good too. God, I trust You to help me to know what to say. I want to be wise about the words I use. Thank You. Amen.

———— **Think about it!** ————

How can God help you choose the right words?

Jesus Helps When I Worry

*"Do not let your heart be troubled. You have
put your trust in God, put your trust in Me also."*
JOHN 14:1

Dear Jesus, I know You want me just to be a kid and not
worry. You said that we shouldn't let our hearts be troubled.
So when I worry, I will trust You to take care of it for me.
I will give all my worries to You. When something bothers
me and I keep thinking about it, will You remind me not to
worry? I know You are with me. I love You, Jesus! Amen.

---— **Think about it!** ---—

Are your worries ever so big
that they keep you up at night?

God Helps Me to Be Brave

With Your help I can go against many soldiers.
PSALM 18:29

Dear God, people do brave things every day. They stand up for what they believe in and fight for what you know is right. That is how I want to be. Bravery doesn't come from being grown up or important. It comes from putting our trust in You. Heavenly Father, I want to be one of Your brave helpers, now and always. Please make me strong to stand up for whatever is good and right. Amen.

--- **Think about it!** ---

In what ways are you brave?

God Helps Me to Be Peaceful

"You will keep the man in perfect peace whose mind is kept on You, because he trusts in You."
Isaiah 26:3

Dear God, bedtime is one of the best times because it is so peaceful. The house is quiet, I'm cozy in bed, and that is when I say my prayers and think about You. You promise that I can feel peaceful not just at bedtime but anytime. Feeling peaceful comes from trusting You and keeping my mind on You. Help me to remember that. Thank You for all the peaceful times that we share together. Amen.

Think about it!

What is peace? And where does it come from?

God Comforts Me

When my worry is great within me,
Your comfort brings joy to my soul.
PSALM 94:19

Dear God, if my mind is busy and I can't sleep, I will trust You to help me rest. I know that You will comfort me. If I think about how much You love me, that helps me to relax. When I trust that You and Your angels watch over me, it helps me feel safe when I sleep. Thank You, God, for being my comforter. Wrap me up warm with Your love. Amen.

Think about it!

Does God help to comfort you
and calm your worries?

God Wipes Away My Tears

"God will take away all their tears."
REVELATION 21:4

Dear God, everybody cries sometimes, and You have a promise about that too—You promise to take away our tears. I'm glad that when I cry it lasts only a little while. You love me, and I think when You see me cry, it makes You sad too. When I am sad, please remind me to think about You. Help me to trust that You will wipe away my tears and make me happy again. Amen.

Think about it!

How does it feel to know that
when you're sad, God's sad too?

God Rewards My Patience

*But they who wait upon the Lord will get
new strength. They will rise up with wings
like eagles. They will run and not get tired.
They will walk and not become weak.*

Isaiah 40:31

Dear God, trusting You means waiting for You to do something. Waiting can be hard at times, but You promise that learning to be patient will make me a better person. Patience helps me to get along well with others. It helps me to be strong in hard times. I need to remember that while I am waiting, You are working on Your wonderful plans for me. Will You help me to be more patient, God? Amen.

Think about it!

How can you be more patient?

God Is Trustworthy Now and Forever

"Know then that the Lord your God is God, the faithful God. He keeps His promise and shows His loving-kindness to those who love Him and keep His Laws, even to a thousand family groups in the future."

DEUTERONOMY 7:9

Dear God, the Bible is filled with stories about people trusting Your promises. You never broke a promise. You always did exactly what You said. I am learning so much about Your promises. I understand that they are for right now, for me and for my family. If I have kids someday, Your promises are for them too. Thank You, God! Now, here is *my* promise to You: I will trust You forever. Amen.

—————————— **Think about it!** ——————————

What is your favorite Bible story
about God and His promises?

GOD IS MINE FOREVER

There Is Only One God

"I am the Lord, and there is no other.
There is no God besides Me."
ISAIAH 45:5

Dear God, I believe with all my heart that You are the one and only God. Nothing is bigger, stronger, or better than You, and still You are never too busy for a little kid like me. I love that about You. You always have time for me. You stay with me day and night, watch over me, and help me. Oh God, I love You so much! Thank You for being my heavenly Father forever. Amen.

—— **Think about it!** ——

Do you believe with all your heart
that God is the One True God?

God's Promises Are Forever

He has remembered His agreement
forever, the promise He made to last
through a thousand families-to-come.
PSALM 105:8

Dear God, thank You for teaching me about Your promises. Please help me to remember them and trust in them every day. Remind me that Your promises are forever. You will never change them or break them. I want to share with my family and friends what I have learned about You. Will You teach me how to do that? I want everyone to know how wonderful You are. I love You, God. Amen.

Think about it!

Do you think it's hard to keep
promises? Why or why not?

God Will Never Leave Me

Those who know Your name will put their trust in You. For You, O Lord, have never left alone those who look for You.
Psalm 9:10

Heavenly Father, one of the best promises is that You will stay with me forever. You made me, and You have been with me every minute of my life. As I grow up, You will be with me all the time. Even when I am very old, You will still be here, loving me and helping me. Please fill up my heart with love for You, and help me to love You more each day. Amen.

Think about it!

What is your favorite Bible promise?

Jesus Is My Savior

*We have seen and are able to say
that the Father sent His Son to save
the world from the punishment of sin.*
1 JOHN 4:14

Dear Jesus, God's Son, You came to save the world from sin. You love me, and You are the best example of how God wants me to live. As I grow up, I want to learn to be more like You. Come into my heart and teach me, Jesus. I know that You are my best friend forever. You are always with me. I will talk to You and trust You to help me. Amen.

――――――――― **Think about it!** ―――――――――

Why did God send Jesus into the world?

Jesus Is Coming Back

"This same Jesus Who was taken from you into heaven will return in the same way you saw Him go up into heaven."
ACTS 1:11

Dear Jesus, You live in heaven with God, but the Bible says that You will come back here someday, and people will see You. You will separate the good people from the bad. A special place will be waiting for everyone who believes in You—a brand-new place where there is nothing but good. Nobody knows when You will come, but it will be a wonderful day. Come, Lord Jesus. I believe in You. Amen.

— **Think about it!** —

What do you think it will be like when Jesus comes back?

MY GOOD-NIGHT PRAYER

God's Promises Are Perfect and Great

Through His shining-greatness and perfect life,
He has given us promises. These promises are of
great worth and no amount of money can buy them.
2 PETER 1:4

Dear God, it's time to say good night. But, before I sleep, I want to thank You for sharing Your promises with me. Help me to remember them all. Every day, please teach me more about You, and every night remind me that I am special because I am Yours. Your promises are perfect and great. Your love for me fills up my heart. I love You too, God, now and forever. Good night, and thank You. Amen.

Think about it!

What was the best thing about your day?

ABOUT THE AUTHOR

Jean Fischer has been writing for children for nearly three decades and has served as an editor with Golden Books. She has written with Thomas Kinkade and John MacArthur and for Adventures in Odyssey. She also wrote for Barbour's Camp Club Girls series. A nature lover, Jean lives in Racine, Wisconsin.

More Bedtime Bible Inspiration for Kids!

365 Classic Bedtime Bible Stories

Beginning with the creation story, "God Creates the Earth," and ending with "In Eternity with God," your children will develop faith in an almighty God who is the same yesterday, today, and forever, while journeying alongside Bible characters like Samuel, Jonah, Esther, David, John the Baptist, Mary, Joseph, and many more. *365 Classic Bedtime Bible Stories* promises to make bedtime reading a delightful learning and faith-building experience!

Hardback / 978-1-63058-380-4 / $19.99